As a Child Grows

by Rosanne Keller
illustrated by Mark Fingar

New Readers Press
Publishing Division of Laubach Literacy International
Syracuse, New York

ISBN 0-88336-511-1

Cover design by Steve Rhodes

Revised 1989 by:

New Readers Press
Publishing Division of
Laubach Literacy International
Box 131, Syracuse, New York 13210
Printed in the United States of America
19 18 17 16 15 14 13 12 11 10

What is a child?

A child is a real person, a human being. A child has needs and wants and dreams. A child is like you and me.

A child is like a flower—growing.

A child is like a baby bird—helpless.

A little plant needs earth to grow in. Good rich earth.

A baby bird needs a nest. A soft, warm nest.

A *child* needs a place to grow, too. A friendly loving place. A place where some things are always the same. A place where the child is an important part of the family.

4

All human beings need, need, need.
The needs are the same.
for you, and me, and a child.

When needs are met, they
are like bright balloons, floating
on the air.

When needs are not met, everything goes flat.

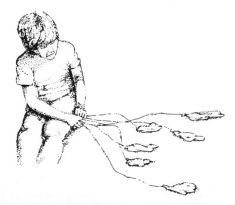

5

This book is about needs. It is about the needs of children. It is about *who* little children are. It is about what they can do.

But mostly, this book is about **love!**

Discipline is part of loving

A child needs a hand to hold. A hand to lead him, to help him, to show him the way. A child needs a hand to hold him close. This is discipline.

Discipline is where love is.

Discipline is limits: "You may not go into the street. I will not let you get hurt."

Discipline is goals: "When you get washed up, I will read you a story."

Discipline is some things always being the same: "We always brush our teeth at night. We never throw our toys."

Discipline is showing how: "This is the way we do dishes. Spoons first."

Discipline is *not* punishment.

When a child acts naughty...

...think about the child's age.

All babies cry. That's how they tell you something is wrong.

All toddlers get into things. This is the way they learn.

All one-year-olds cry when their mothers leave. They are learning love and trust.

All two-year-olds say, "NO." They are showing that they are themselves.

All three-year-olds hit their playmates. They are just learning to share.

All children act naughty sometimes. And so do grown-ups!

...find out why he is unhappy.

Is the child tired? Does he need a nap? Is he hungry or thirsty? Is he bored? Find out why he is unhappy. Then help him.

Get his mind off the problem. Give him something else to do that is fun or exciting. Do something *with* him. Maybe he is just lonely.

. . . discipline him, don't punish him.

Don't spank, slap or jerk him. Don't close him in a room alone. These are punishments. Punishment and discipline are not the same. Children learn different things from punishment and discipline.

What does a child learn from *punishment?*

"I cannot go in the street—or I will get a spanking."

"I cannot grab toys from my friends—or my mother will spank me."

"I have to clean up—or my dad will yell at me!"

"I have to do so many things so that Mom and Dad won't get mad at me!!!"

What does a child learn from *discipline?*

"I cannot go in the street—because you love me too much to let me get hurt."

"I cannot grab toys from my friends—because I don't like to make them upset."

"I have to clean up—because it looks so nice when it is neat."

"I have to do so many things because I am growing up!"

Try to be understanding and firm and cheerful. And praise a child when he does good. Praise is a part of discipline, too.

When a child grows in the love of discipline, he learns to love. He learns to take care of things. He learns to care for others. He learns to discipline himself.

Self-discipline is the goal of discipline.

Self-discipline is the mark of being grown up. This is what we want a child to become: a loving, caring, self-disciplined grown-up!

You can help make this happen! You can give a child a hand to hold. You can give a child a place to grow.

With your hands, you can lead a child. You can help him.

You can show the way.

Then, the child can get on with the work of growing up.

A child's work is

Play and discipline go hand in hand.

You can help a child. You can give her a
beautiful gift. You can do this even if it is just for
a day, or an evening, or a weekend, or a lifetime.
You can give your time, your love, your help. The
best gift is yourself.

Remember, for a time, a little person's life is in
your hands.

Different ages like different things

A child needs a place where he can play. A place where there is discipline so he will feel safe. A friendly, loving place. A place where he can be himself.

But different ages like and need different things, too. Here are some things children like. Here are some things you can do. Here are some things children *need* at different ages.

Listen to what each child says. Each child is talking to you.

Hi! I'm a newborn baby...

So tiny, so soft,
so helpless!
I'm just waking up to
    the world,
    slowly, with
    wide eyes.

I can

hear	burp
see	blink
taste	frown
feel	turn my head
startle	smell
spit up	**cry!**

Sometimes I scare you when I cry.
Sometimes I make you feel helpless!

I need

    to hear soft sounds like singing, soft talking

    to see smiling faces

    to have my head held up

    to be dry and warm

    to be burped gently after eating.

I like

    to sleep

    to drink warm milk

    to be wrapped up snug in my blankets

    to be held close

    to be patted

    to be cuddled

    to be left alone when I sleep.

You can

    rock me

    sing to me

    talk to me softly.

No loud noises, please.
No quick moving, please.

Hi!
I'm an infant - only 3 to 6
months old...
So wiggly, so smiley, and
still so helpless!

I can

  look at things
  listen
  hold my head up
  reach for—and grab—things
  suck my fingers
  try to sit up
  roll over
  smile.

I need
> to be hugged and cuddled
> to sleep a lot
> to be sung to
> to be played with
> to be warm and dry.

I like
> to kick and wiggle
> to be jiggled gently
> to be cuddled
> to see pretty colors
> to make gurgles and coos
> to look at my hands
> to smile.

You can
> take me for walks in a stroller
> sing and talk to me
> smile at me
> show me rattles, mobiles, toys
> play a music box for me.

No rough play, please.
Watch that I don't roll off things.
Keep small objects out of my reach.

Hi! I'm a pre-toddler, 7 to 12 months old...

So loud,
    so bouncy,
        so cuddly!

I can
> pull up to standing
> sit up well
> make lots of sounds
> understand some words
> eat well—if you feed me
> crawl or creep.

Sometimes I scare you when I climb and fall.
Sometimes you get tired because I'm always
    on the go.

I need

> to be played with
>
> to be dry
>
> to touch, smell, feel, hear, and taste my world
>
> to be watched all the time.

I like

> to play with my toys
>
> to put things in my mouth
>
> to drop things from my high chair!
>
> to play pat-a-cake
>
> to bang things together
>
> to tear paper
>
> to crawl and pull up.

You can

> sing to me
>
> play nursery-rhyme or song games
>
> show me cloth books
>
> pick up the things I drop!
>
> give me pots and pans to play with
>
> let me tear old newspapers
>
> walk me around (while you hold my hands).

Never leave me alone.

Keep small objects out of my reach.

Keep cleaning things (soap, powders) up high.

Hi! I'm a toddler, 1 year old...
So full of zip, so into
everything,
So big...
yet so
little.

I can
use my hands well
use a spoon
take off my clothes
walk

help pick up
stack blocks
understand simple words
talk with one or two words.

I need
> to be played with
> to take a nap or two a day
> to be dry
> to find out about things...show me!
> to be watched all the time.

I like
> to go, go, go!
> to shout
> to get into everything
> to tear books!
> to put everything in my mouth
> to push and pull toys
> to put things into something.

You can
> sing with me—I like to try
> show me short books
> give me a big box to play in
> tie a string on something I can pull
> give me a big can and things to put in it
> give me a spoon and a pie pan
> chase me and catch me.

Never leave me alone.
Watch that I don't hurt myself or break
things.

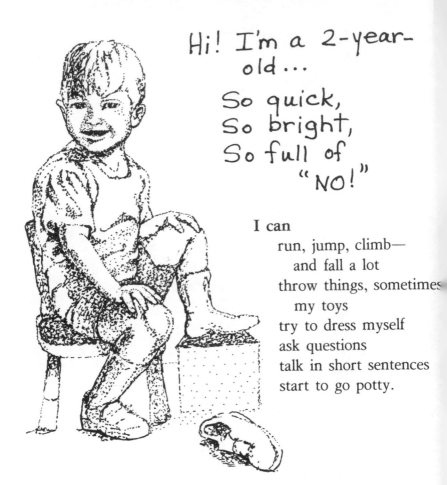

Hi! I'm a 2-year-old...

So quick,
So bright,
So full of
"NO!"

I can

> run, jump, climb—
>   and fall a lot
> throw things, sometimes
>   my toys
> try to dress myself
> ask questions
> talk in short sentences
> start to go potty.

Sometimes you can't understand what I say.
    I cry.
Sometimes I don't understand what you say.
    You cry!
Sometimes you feel like wringing my neck!
But remember, I'm still pretty little.

I need

> to be told I am good
> to be told you are proud of me
> to play, play, play—indoors and outdoors
> to be held and loved when I'm hurt or scared
> to know what I may and may not do
> to have help when I'm angry.

I like

> to run, climb, jump, and fall
> to draw with a pencil
> to be read to, the same books over and over
> to play in water
> to play outdoors—I may wander off, though!
> to dig with a shovel
> to ride on big toys
> to tell you things.

You can

> play with me, chase me, play hide and seek
> read to me, and sing with me
> let me "wash dishes" in soapy water
> ask me questions, "What's this? What's that?"
> answer my questions
> give me boxes to get into.

Never leave me alone.

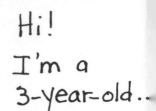

Hi!
I'm a
3-year-old..

So full of talk,
So nice to be with
So full of question

I can
    run fast without falling
    do what you tell me—
      sometimes!
    talk pretty well
    ask many questions
    tell about things I do or see
    share—sometimes
    take turns—sometimes
    go to the potty—mostly.
I may cry or whine a lot.
There are so many things I
    don't understand.

I need

to be told how big I am

to be praised when I am good

to be loved when I'm hurt or scared

to know what I may and may not do

to know when you are pleased with me

to have the same naptime and bedtime
every day.

I like

to dance, run, twirl around, do somersaults

to ride a tricycle

to hear stories about myself

to decide some things for myself

to be read to

to draw and paint

to please you.

You can

play musical games with me—Farmer in the
Dell

read and tell stories to me

let me decide between two things to do

let me draw, paint, and color

talk *with* me

let me help you, then praise me

take me for walks

let me do as much as I can for myself.

Never leave me alone outdoors.

Hi!
I'm a 4-
year-old . . .
So tall now,
So full of
     pretend,
So full of
"I can do it
        myself!"

I can
> turn a somersault, hop on
> one foot, climb a tree,
> ride a tricycle
> throw a ball—or a toy
> talk *with* you
> do what you do—or try!
> dress myself
> pick up my room
> help you.

I don't cry so much. I can
talk it out.

I need

    to be played with

    to be read to

    to know what I may and may not do

    to know what is happening—what the plans are

    to be cuddled, loved, and told I'm a good
      person

    to be told you are proud of me.

I like

    to play with sand, water, clay, and mud

    to draw, paint, make things

    to play house, hide and seek, music games

    to pretend and dress up

    to make up stories

    to use grown-up tools—with help.

You can

    let me cut, paste, draw, and color

    make a tent for me with chairs and a blanket

    give me grown-up clothes to dress up in

    read to me

    let me help you

    teach me how to use things

    let me do things for myself.

Don't tell me scary stories.

Hi! I'm a 5-year-old...
no longer
a baby,
ready for
school,
I'm a person!
I'm almost
all
grown up!

I can
     play lots of games—
       and learn more
     sing lots of songs
     talk, talk, talk
     play well with friends
     mind you
     help around the house
     help with smaller children.

You can trust me—
     most of the time.
I can be your friend.

I need

comfort when I'm hurt or lonely

lots of play

to be told you love me

to hear you tell others about the good in me

to be praised when I've been helpful

to see what a fine person I am.

I like

to ride a bike

to run and play hard

to look at books—and try to read!

to play games

to make things—cut and paste

to have real jobs

to do things on my own.

You can

go on hikes or bike rides with me—on safe trails

let me play with my friends—with rules

read to me

play games with me

help me make things

give me little jobs, then praise me

teach me songs

talk with me.

Safety rules for play

For a baby:

    Be sure toys are clean.

    Don't wear sharp or pointed things.

    No toys with small parts that come off.

    Never leave the baby alone.

For a child:

    All toys should be bigger than a child's two fists.

    No tiny, sharp, or pointed things.

    No jumping from high places.

    No plastic bags.

    Check to see if toys are broken or unsafe.

    Keep shoelaces tied and belts fastened.

    No playing in the street.

    Never leave the child alone.

This little person has never happened before and will never happen again. And for a time, this little person's life is in your hands.

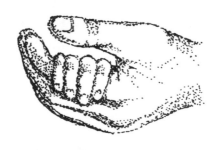

When needs are met, a child is given wings. When needs are met, a child can become what he or she was meant to be. You can help give a child wings.

You can help them **fly!**